The Black Man's Intervention Volume 2:

The Onus Is On You

By Aaron Fields

Illustration Cover By: Ezechukwu George Kelvin

ISBN: 978-1-953962-379

Something To Think About Before You Read

In order for the black man to know himself, he must know what's going on around him

------------Aaron Fields

Table Of Contents:

Chapter 1 Avoid Victimhood…………………………………………………1

Chapter 2 Work On The Micro Before The Macro……………………………..3

Chapter 3 Don't Be Pathetic………………5

Chapter 4 How To Make Progress In The Black Community?…………………………7

Chapter 5 The Man Must Have Authority ……………………………9

Chapter 6 Why Is There Confusion In The Black Community?......................................11

Chapter 7 Avoid The Traps……………………………13

Chapter 8 Baby Mama Drama……………………………15

Chapter 9 Black Is Not A Culture…………………………………17

Chapter 10 Is The Bible The "White Man's Book"?……………………………18

Chapter 11 Don't Teach Victimhood……………………………19

Chapter 12 Other Demographics Don't Care About You…………………………20

Chapter 13 How To Regain Power?……………………………21

Chapter 14 Stop Being Too Inclusive……………………………22

Chapter 15 Control Your Own Narrative……………………23

Word From the Author

It's important for black men to understand the impact of their presence in this society. Black men are required to lead their communities and households, as well as to be perceptive to their surroundings. More importantly, black men must take pride in raising and guiding their children. Why? Well, because the black man's child is an exact replication of him, especially if he has a son.

One of the greatest things a black man can help create in this world is a child. That's why it's important for black men to be cognizant of the type of women they impregnate. It is up to us as black men to recognize that the women we father children with will mirror our own image. How we treat our women and raise our children will be a direct representation of us.

Why is the onus on us? Ultimately, society doesn't want to hear black men voice their complaints. Is society set up to place black men at the bottom of the totem pole? Yes, to a certain degree. However, that doesn't mean we have to be susceptible to what society thinks of us and walk around with a self-defeated mentality. Is the system rigged? Given that the system is not in their favor, black men must learn how to adapt and improve their life circumstances and avoid blaming others.

Avoid Victimhood

If you take on the role of being a victim, it will make you seem powerless. Just because you're a black man in this society, it doesn't mean you have to conform to a self-victimization mentality. Many people in the black community have a habit of playing the victim.

Unfortunately, many black people in our dysfunctional community suffer from entitlement issues. What do I mean by that? African Americans often believe they are entitled to what they want, and any punishment they receive is because of racism. To be clear, there are certain individuals and authority figures who harbor negative views of black people. However, it's not wise for a black man to always believe that he's never in the wrong. Every once in a while, you have to be honest with yourself and look at yourself in the mirror.

The lack of a father figure in the lives of many black men has affected their ability to respect authority. A lack of paternal guidance often results in black men displaying more feminine characteristics. Without proper fathering, black men focus more on their emotions rather than on finding solutions.

What are your thoughts on the victimhood mentality and explain to me how this way of thinking can affect your life?

_____

_____

_____

_____

_____

_____

_____

_____

_____

_____

Work On The Micro Before The Macro

What exactly do I mean when I say work on the micro before the macro? Well, in order to make societal changes on a macrocosmic level, the black man must work on himself as opposed to looking at these other demographics to change. Before coming up with a macrocosmic plan, it's important to look at yourself in the mirror and figure out what you can do as an individual first. If you can't govern yourself, or preside over your household, you can't establish order.

If black men don't learn how to change themselves first, it's going to be impossible to make macro-level changes. If black men come together and choose to act and think in a more constructive way, they could use the system to their advantage. Again, it must start with the black man.

Please save yourself the stress and stop going back and forth with these other demographics. Stop trying to guilt them into changing laws and policies. Stop depicting yourself as the victim. Why? Well, because society doesn't believe that black men are victims.

So, what are some things black men can do? Black men must learn how to elevate and empower themselves. It's necessary for Black men to learn how to make wiser decisions and be more self-controlled. Black men must also develop great awareness and a great understanding of the things that are going on around them.

In order to make societal changes on a macrocosmic level, what are some things you need to improve on or change from within?

_____

_____

_____

_____

_____

_____

_____

_____

_____

_____

_____

_____

_____

_____

_____

_____

Don't Be Pathetic

Unfortunately, there are too many unintelligent individuals in the black community who intentionally seek to decrease their mental capacity instead of aiming to enhance their standard of living. Unfortunately, many of the poor decisions black men make end up becoming a direct reflection of their community. Because of the dysfunctional culture, the black man looks pathetic.

Please keep in mind that in life, no one ever respects someone that is pathetic. Please understand that when society views the black man as someone who is pathetic, that means society doesn't respect him. It's very important that black men as a collective understand this concept.

Luckily, there are some black men out there who come up with solutions to their problems. Yes, this world can be hard to navigate, but it doesn't make it any easier when you're constantly blaming everyone else for your shortcomings. Believe it or not, a lot of you guys can succeed in this world. You just don't believe in yourself.

In order to achieve any level of success in this world, you need to create goals. Sadly, one of the major problems we have in the black community is that many black men don't believe in themselves. Believe it or not, many young black men have high aspirations, but unfortunately, many of them get discouraged. As a result, many young black men become bitter, angry, and resentful because they didn't stick to their goals. In life, you can't blame society for your own lack of discipline. You must find a path to victory despite the obstacles.

Are there any goals you would like to achieve in this world? Is there anything or anyone that is discouraging you or stopping you from achieving your goals?

_____

_____

_____

_____

_____

_____

_____

_____

_____

_____

_____

How To Make Progress In The Black Community?

A major reason the black community is not making progress in this society is because many of them are low-level thinkers. Why do I say that? Well, it's because most black people walk around in this society feeling defeated and blameless. Black people attribute their failures to "the system," but for some strange reason, they struggle to accept that their inadequate individual and parental performance is a major cause.

Most black parents are too busy teaching their children how to be victims of the system instead of teaching them how to use the system to their advantage. For example, it's important for black parents to inform their children about how the school system operates. It's vital for black parents to understand that the school system doesn't exist to enlighten you. The school system indoctrinates you. When a black child is in these schools, it's important for them to know how to use certain parts of the system to their advantage. The problem with black people is that many of them want to be validated by the system. Instead of trying to overcome the system, they want to ingratiate themselves in it. It is apparent that black parents rely too much on the educational system as opposed to taking the initiative to teach their own children.

The reason behind black people's emotional turmoil is their excessive effort to seek acceptance from America. That's why most black people get very upset and emotionally sensitive when they perceive something as racist. Please keep in mind that the United States of America will never accept black people, especially the black man. Once you understand this concept and no longer require acceptance from this society, your course of action and decisions will be much better.

What are some other ways black people can make progress in their community? What are some ideas and strategies black men in particular can do to elevate their people?

_____

_____

_____

_____

_____

_____

_____

_____

_____

_____

_____

_____

_____

_____

The Man Must Have Authority

Just because you're a present father doesn't mean your kid will automatically become a moral person. However, if you are active in your child's life, it will most likely lead to better outcomes. It's important for the black man to eliminate any negative variables that can negatively affect his life. For example, black men as a collective must make sure that they're impregnating the right woman.

Sadly, in the black community, so many black men are getting random women pregnant. It's essential for black men to be diligent in deciding which type of woman they want to carry their offspring. Why do you have to be meticulous? Well, it's because the most important thing that a black man will ever help create in this world is a child. That's why it's important for black men to value their sperm and stop ejaculating into these random women that they don't even know.

Why is society trying to destroy masculinity and fatherhood in the black community? It's because they know that when a man has authority over his spouse; he has authority over his kids. Women are beautiful and deserving of love and respect. However, black men must acknowledge that women are emotional beings, with limited capacity to think and act on a macro level. Now are there exceptions to the rule? Yes, but most women will do whatever it takes to survive, even if it means conforming to societal expectations. That's why it's important for black men who are spiritual, astute and upstanding to take back control of their household and their community.

Something To Think About

One of the most crucial periods in a young boy's life takes place between the ages of ten and fifteen. Why? Well, if you think about it, that's usually when the young black boy develops a better understanding of everything that's going on around him.

Puberty is an important stage for a young man. Not only are his hormones changing, but he's also exploring the world around him. At this stage, most young men are also trying to figure out what group they belong to and where they fit into society. Believe it or not, the ages between ten and fifteen are usually a period when the young man may rebel against authority and his parents, especially if the young man lacks a father figure and comes from a single mother household.

*Why are most young black men rebelling against their mothers and fathers? Read chapter 6.

Why Is There Confusion In The Black Community?

From a spiritual perspective, the rebellion of women against men in the black community is due to the majority of black men rebelling against the most high God. As a result of the women rebelling against the men, the children are rebelling against the parents. Are you noticing the trickle-down effect?

The reason there is confusion in the black community is because no one is following the chain of command (God, Christ, Man, Woman, Child). In order to make progress in the black community, we must follow and respect the chain of command. If we choose not to, we will continue to have major problems in our community.

Failure to follow the chain of command by the black community increases the likelihood of conforming to society's toxic ideologies. The reason the onus is primarily on the black man is because it's his job to operate on a higher level. It's also the black man's job to not fall prey to gender war propaganda. That's why it's important for black men to stop arguing and going back and forth with women. Please keep in mind that arguing with women is nothing but a distraction. Society encourages you to argue with women to divert your attention from understanding what's happening around you. Your goal as a black man is to maintain order and develop a sense of peace in your life. Therefore, once you have peace and a great understanding of the world around you, you'll be able to teach and guide the women and children in your life.

What are your thoughts on the chain of command (God, Christ, Man, Woman, Child)? Is the black community following the chain of command? If the black man is not following the chain of command, who is he following? Is he following himself? Is he following the woman? Give me your thoughts.

_____

_____

_____

_____

_____

_____

_____

_____

_____

_____

_____

_____

_____

_____

Avoid The Traps

Is there some level of racism in this society? Yes, there is. Is the system rigged? Yes, it is (to a certain degree). Now that you know that the system is rigged to make the black man fail, what actions will you take to change it? Since the system is out to get you, why are you selling drugs? Why are you getting involved in gang activity? Why are you partaking in self-destructive behavior? Why are you going back and forth with women? If the system is out to get you, why do you keep falling into the same traps?

Learn effective strategies to thrive in a society that opposes black men. Yes, many young black men are in the prison system. What is the black man going to do about it? Well, for starters, black men as a collective must reject and stop embracing criminality and this "thug life culture".

What else does the black man need to let go of? Besides rejecting the drug/gang culture and alcoholism, black men should also refrain from idolizing women. Speaking of women, black men must also stop mistreating them. Anything that is negative and hindering the black man from succeeding, he must let go of it.

Sometimes, in order to succeed in life, you must embrace solitude. Please keep in mind that there is nothing wrong with being by yourself for an extended period. Don't succumb to peer pressure and involve yourself with people or groups that don't care about your happiness and wellbeing. Why? Well, because most people that come into your life will not have your best interest at heart.

Now am I saying you should never go to events, parties, or spend time with women or your homeboys? No, I'm not suggesting that because engaging in those activities healthily is acceptable. Just make sure you have your priorities in order. It's important to always strive for overall health and stability by taking care of yourself financially, physically, mentally, and spiritually.

Baby Mama Drama

Now what if the mother of your child is becoming a gatekeeper between you and your child? What if the woman is trying to prevent you from raising your kid? What if the woman doesn't respect fatherhood?

Gentlemen, I hate to break it to you, but if the mother of your child is making your life a living hell, you have to deal with the consequences of getting the wrong woman pregnant. Why? Well, because you decided to get her pregnant, you now have to deal with her nonsense for at least eighteen years.

Since you're dealing with baby mama drama, you must find ways to maintain your sanity. While you're doing that, you must look at your child or your children as an investment. If possible, just focus on the health and wellbeing of your kids instead of going back and forth with the mother. Use the court system to your advantage if the mother of your child is self-destructive, difficult, and stopping you from being involved in your child's life. Many of these women out here are vicious and extremely wicked. Therefore, it's your job as a man to stand up to her and run her through the court system, especially if she's harming your children. Believe it or not, a lot of women in this society are not wife and mother material.

Questions For the Black Man To Think About

Why are you getting random women pregnant?

Why are you bringing children into this world if you have no intentions on raising them?

Why are you allowing your children to grow up in a toxic and confused environment?

Why are you bringing more chaos and confusion into your community?

Black Is Not A Culture

Although our community frequently uses the term "black," it is essential to understand that it only refers to a color, not a race/ethnicity. Believe it or not, the term "black" does not mean race, culture, or place of origin. The term "black" is only a label and a term that is used in the western society to describe the indigenous population (African Americans).

Why is the term "black" being used as a label against the indigenous population? Well, it's because western society does not want the native black people to know their origins and where they come from. Instead of having their own distinct culture, most black people will adopt the cultural standards of society. Even though these other demographics don't care about them, black people rely on them to teach them about their own history.

Do black people, as a collective, have a real culture? Well, before you say yes, ask yourself these questions. Do black people like working together? Do black people have a code of ethics? Does the black community have a set of customs, values, and principles that they adhere to? Do black people have a good understanding of their history and where they actually come from?

Is The Bible The "White Man's Book"?

Why do the vast majority of black people call the bible "The White Man's Book"? Well, if you ask me, I believe it stems from the image of the Caucasian version of Jesus Christ being used as a psychological manipulation tactic towards black people in the church system. If we're being honest, most black people have not read the entire bible. In fact, if you read the bible, you'll notice that the bible has nothing to do with the Caucasian man presiding over the bible.

The Bible is not viewed as the White Man's Book because its laws and commandments contradict the laws and ideologies of modern society.. With that being said, I understand why most black people believe the bible is the white man's book. Unfortunately, the bible was a tool to support imperialism when the white man came into power.

While more people have knowledge about the bible now, there are also more agnostics and atheists. That's why it's important to read the bible in its entirety and for your own understanding. Don't allow false propagandas and psychological manipulation tactics to control your way of thinking.

11

Don't Teach Victimhood

Gentlemen, please don't allow yourself to fall into this victimhood mentality. Make sure little black boys don't fall prey to this victimhood mentality as well. The promotion of victimhood in the black community to young black men is an attempt to portray them as weak and replace them with black women as the authority figure.

Sadly, in the black community, most black mothers are teaching their sons how to be fearful and emotional victims. Therefore, as the son gets older, he exudes more feminine traits because he has the spirit of the woman in him. That's why the onus is on the black man to have authority over his family so he can take back control of his community and his household. In order to do this, the black man must get his life in order.

How does the black man take back control of his household? How does the black man gain his respect back? How can black men be leaders and authority figures in the community? Well, for starters, we must put more time and focus on spiritual things. We must practice and incorporate self-discipline and self-motivation into our lives. As it pertains to women, black men must be more mindful and meticulous about the women they interact with and impregnate.

12

Other Demographics Don't Care About You

Most of these other demographics don't care about black men. They don't care about black-on-black crime; they don't care about black men getting killed by cops. They don't care about the overall health and wellbeing of the black man. Most of these other groups are just trying to appear concerned to feel significant when it comes to understanding the challenges black men face.

As soon as you establish you are self-reliant and free from a subordinate mentality to these other demographics; they will turn on you. As soon as you show these other demographics that you're a man and you are solution oriented, they will show so much animosity and hatred towards you.

A major reason other demographics don't care about black men is because they try to conflate the issues involving the black man with their own issues. Whenever something bad happens to a black man, the other demographics want to use his plight so they can make everything about them. For example, when a black man gets shot by the cops, the media will attempt to use the black man's plight to promote homosexuality, lesbianism, the transgender community, feminism, and globalism.

How To Regain Power?

Other demographics leverage the black man's struggle to promote their agenda because they understand their energy is not as potent as the black man's. Why is that? Well, if I had to take a guess, perhaps it's a divine gift that the most high God has blessed us with.

In life, there is good energy, and there is destructive energy. As it pertains to black men, it's important to show good energy. If black men, as a collective, attempted to generate more positive energy into the universe, we will regain power and control. However, in order for this to happen, the onus is on us as black men to get our lives in order.

No disrespect to these other demographics, but they are not the answer to the black man's salvation. That's why it's important for black men to put their faith in God and not in this society. Like I said earlier, these other demographics don't give a damn about you. In order for the black man to improve himself and his people, it will have to take a great deal of time and effort. Whether you want to accept this or not, marching and protesting will not solve the black man's issues. Most of these people you see out there marching, protesting, and screaming "black Lives Matter" don't have an actual solution to the problem.

Stop Being Too Inclusive

Although there are many young intelligent black men, most of them are also confused. Why are so many black men confused? It escapes the understanding of many black men that they are being used by other demographics to further their own agenda.

The problem with many of these black men is that they are too inclusive. Why is the black man trying to include everyone? Have you noticed that these other demographics don't want to include black men when it comes to fulfilling their own agenda?

These other demographics will only include black men in their agenda only if black men conform to their ideologies. In order for black men to be their allies, black men have to stay in their lane and know their place. Their preference is for black men to work as security guards. Other demographics don't want black men to think for themselves or have their own entity. It's important for black men to understand that there is no need to be inclusive with other people that don't give a damn about you.

Control Your Own Narrative

It's important for black men to not let others create a narrative about them. The only person who can control your narrative is you. Now keep in mind there will be other people in this society that will try to embellish or create a false narrative about you. However, in order to overcome or create a counterattack, the black man must be the autobiographer. In addition to that, the black man also needs to learn how to respect himself and start developing positive habits.

Always remember that your life is a story, and you are the main character. It's time to take the reins of your life and start deciding for yourself and taking responsibilities for your actions. Yes, life can be scary sometimes and we're all going to make mistakes because none of us are perfect, but that doesn't mean you should give up on yourself.

Stop dwelling on the past and stop looking at these other demographics for guidance and support. In order to take a chance on yourself, you must learn how to think for yourself. Don't put yourself in a situation that will cause you to fall short of your goals. Sometimes, in order to elevate your level of existence and manifest your gifts, you might have to change your mindset. Why? Well, because your old way of thinking was making you feel stuck and afraid.

I believe that many black men are talented and gifted. Please don't sit around and let life pass you by. It is not acceptable for a black man to be unproductive. I hope and pray that the most high God helps you rise above your excuses and overcome your demons. It is imperative that you become the author of your own story. I can't make you do it because you have to be the one that has to make that conscious choice. Please keep in mind that life is short. Instead of being reactionary to other people and their views, I'd much rather see you guys spend more time

pursuing the things that will maximize your level of peace in this world.

Notes

All of us have lived different experiences that have transformed our lives; however, it is important that you use your hardships in life as a platform for success, fulfillment, and peace. We've all made mistakes and none of us are perfect. Yet, when we know better, we should do better and learn from our past mistakes.